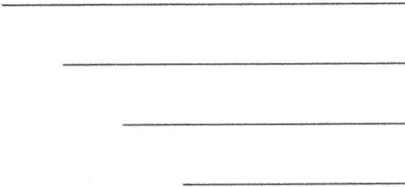

DIE HAPPY or DIE TRYING

J. Hol

poetry and musings
about just making it by however you can
however you want
however works

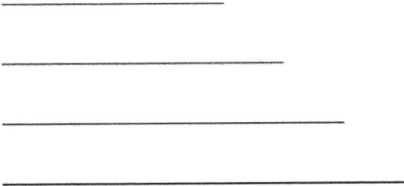

All writings written,
conceived, and sporadically
executed by J. Hol.

ISBN: 978-1-955814-62-1

SCIS
SORT
AIL:P
RESS
COVER & BOOK DESIGN BY BRIAN FUCHS
SCISSORTAILPRESS.COM

★

Dedicated to you, no pressure

Hi and fuck you, I'm tired of this book.

sorry -

still fuck you,
but also

thank you.

For reading or skimming or whatever you're
doing here
I'm just tired.
Writing a book is hard.
Reading your own dumb lines
over and over
again and again
to make sure they're presented well,
presented like they are in your head,
and mean well,
mean what they mean in your head,
and mean anything at all
is hard -
really hard.
And then of course -
spelling
and punctuation,
and grammar,
and finding the time
and not hating it
and trying,
and retrying,
and retrying -

but I think I did it,

so thanks

5$/each reward to anyone who finds a spelling error that isn't intentional - email me with proof - jholgate993@gmail.com -

TABLE OF CONTENTS

hey, hi, hello

"...but I have heard of you."

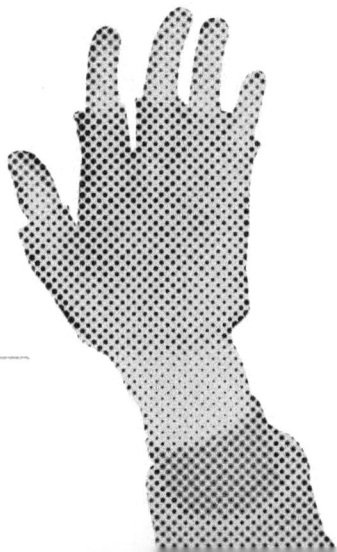

SOME THINGS

I don't know what to tell you.
I don't know what I should tell you.
I don't know what you want to know.

I'm restless
I don't like loud noises, which means I can
scare easily
My feet smell worse than the rest of my body
combined
I like flowers and wish I could identify more of
them by sight
I hate feeling small and I'll hate you if you
make me feel small
My favorite color and food change regularly
I usually tell people it's dark green and Mac n'
Cheese so the conversation ends there.
I'm comfortable in a crowd or in front of one,
as long as I don't have to act like myself
I'm allergic to horses so I could never go to the
petting zoo as a child

I think about that more than I should
My shoe size will never make sense to me
I smoke cigarettes and do drugs
I have the worst vision out of almost anyone I
know
I read the entire Bible once to see what all the
fuss was about
It didn't live up to the hype
Spoiler Alert: Jesus dies
I drink a lot of water
I think I want to have children

Last night I burped so venously I almost
vomited
I don't like hospitals
I don't know what venously means or if I used
it correctly in that line above
I'm both a dog or cat person and think it's
stupid that people make you choose
I'd choose either over the person asking that
stupid question
I like art, but usually don't like other people
who like art
My favorite holiday is Holloween
I always misspelled Halloween as Holloween
I don't know why, it just makes more sense to
me I guess
My girlfriend is currently constipated
She wouldn't like that I told you that
Everything I know about cars I learned from
UBER

Nature seems like it's always trying to kill me
I like gay people and for a time thought I was
gay myself
I'm not a good cook
I wear baggy clothes because I'm
uncomfortable with my body
I haven't gotten a proper haircut in years
I broke my hip once
I mishear things a lot

I like to write.

I want to be happy.

And that's it.

LIVING

And so he sat –
Like a hamster learning Chinese
Knowing full well
He'll never get this
He'll never be a part
He'll never even enjoy it
He'll never understand any of it
He'll never know the tricks of lingo
He does not belong
But here he is
Motionless
Soundless
Synthetic nodding
Affirming smile
Two thumbs up
Way up
Way up
Hands in the air
Does he care?

Unfortunately,
yes.

And so this is life
An here he is –
Living

UFO / IFO

You ever think about how
Identifying a UFO as a UFO makes it not a UFO
Read that again
I'll wait

-   -

Got it? Good.

So technically –
Because even though the **U** in UFO means
"**unidentified**," you still identified it as
something that is **unidentifiable** therefore
giving it an **identity** and making it no longer **U**
aka unidentified
Like it or not - it is now an
IFO - identified flying object
Weird right (or I'm dumb - unsure)
There's a lot of things like that in this world
though
Like how "**buildings**" are already **built**
And all the cow**boys** are old as shit now

The universe is strange like that
Our world is so understood, labeled, manicured,
pedicured, and figured out to make total,
scheduled sense
That things start to make no sense at all
Which gives birth to the bilateral reality that is
funny in a way
We try so hard to understand
But it doesn't want us to
It wants us to wonder and it pushes us to do so -
little linguistic burn holes in the fabric of it all
Almighty jokes we call irony, comedy, idiocy
I'm sure you have examples in your own life
I do –
I was so worried I was starting to lose my hair
I won't look good bald
I don't look good now
So I won't look good bald

For months
Panicked
I took these weird overhead photos and videos
peering into my scalp
My king's crown
Zooming in and out
Collecting my depressing data
Studying my brain from the outside
Making sure its fuzzy shell was intact – was
there at all
And then –
Funnily enough
I was diagnosed with cancer
And was almost treated with chemotherapy
Where I would absolutely lose all my hair
My king's crown, court, castle, the lot
The universe was trying to warn me something
was wrong
She said – you have cancer!
And I said – oh shit, am I balding?

But I didn't have to get chemotherapy after all
And I still have all my hair
Kingdom intact
I'm doing well now – a story for another time
The universe spared me the lesson
She chose not to be so cruel
To have a less committed sense of humor
She showed me her hand
I misread
Called her bluff
Fucked it up
But, she did not condemn me for it
I don't know what I learned
in our cosmic little poker game
But I'm still holding my cowboys
Atop my little IFO

VEGETARIAN

When I was 22 a doctor told me in order to
stop being anemic -
(cold all the time / general shittiness)
I could either take iron pills the size of my
knuckles
or
Eat a cheeseburger once a week
Determined;
I picked up the pills before I left his office
Then promptly drove to the nearest McDonalds

My eyes were always bigger than my morals
anyway

PINK'S HOTDOGS

Here I sit
Bleeding
In the city of angels
(you know the one)
Locked in a bathroom
(you probably don't know the one)
A porcelain prison
Because of the shitty lock
On the shitty door
At the not so shitty hot dog place
No poem
Just my life
Or maybe a Yelp review
Can't post yet -
Should save battery
Don't know how long it'll be
The heavy breathing man beating the door
senseless with a screwdriver on the other side
doesn't seem to speak any English
Which I don't mind
But it would be nice to know what's going on

I can only tell it's a screwdriver because he
keeps ramming it through the broken locking
mechanism
Like an inverse view of a violent game of
whack-a-mole
More like stab-a-mole
But that probably won't go over as well at
carnivals
He got me pretty good in the hand when I was
still trying to help unlock the door from within
Hence the bleeding
Now I've given up
And I'm sitting in the toilet writing this instead
With my not bloody hand
It's fine
Of all places to bleed
A bathroom is up there with hospitals and
blood drives

Another man is at the shitty door now
I think he's trying something with the shitty
hinges of the shitty door

Less invasive
But much more noisy
There's an inherent anxiety that comes with
this
Not because I'm locked in here
I'm sure if heavy breather and hinges can't
figure it out they'll call the fire department to
ax the door down or blow it up or something
I'll get out
No no that's not the issue
It's the fact the something on the other side is
trying so feverishly to get in
I know they're trying to help me
And themselves
Because this can't be a great look
But still
The feeling is there
Something literally breaking down a door
while I sit here
On a toilet
In my own shit stench

Bleeding
My shitty door
To my shitty bathroom
My vulnerable little place
Where I piss shit and bleed
Breaking down my door to my bathroom
And they want it so badly
They'll huff and puff and slam and ram to do
so

At least I already ate
It was good

"4 stars: Good food. Horrible bathrooms. Most
anxious piss shit and bleed of my life. Don't
ask."

There's my review
Maybe I can get a free drink out of this or
something?
5 stars if I do

MY FAVORITE ROOM I'VE EVER LIVED IN

Was cramped
But that was ok
It was all I could afford at the time and it was
worth it for the perks
First of all the view
It had this beautiful bay window right in the
front
This window basically spanned the entirety of
the room
Breathtaking
There were other windows too, lots of natural
light could come in
And the music
There was built-in speakers in the room so I
could always play whatever I wanted as loud
as I wanted
The neighbors never seemed to care
They weren't home much
Oh god and the thermostat was so easy to use I
could get that room to whatever temperature

I wanted in record time
And it had these super comfy leather chairs in
there too
Just great –
Built in ashtray
Built in digital clock
Lighting worked great
Plenty of mirrors
Yeah wow
I loved that room
I guess my only complaint would be –

It was a car

THE SLIGHT PAINS OF TODAY ARE THE TRIGGER FINGERS OF TOMORROW

Your body does it's job

So why don't you?

Your body -

Oscillates blood

Filters oxygen

Uses all its delicate senses

Walks and talks and thinks

All the muscles contract and reflex

All the hair grows

And the nails

Both pupils dilate appropriately

Your body does all of these things -

With little to no intervention on your part

You're too busy

Being busy

To all things -

that don't matter

You don't work

Well you "work"

But not like your body

Your entire being is a group project

And you're the asshole that signs his name

but does nothing of worth

I love this body for that -
I can coast through life on my basic -
stadard issue body alone
Until it is unable to pick up my slack any
longer
My hair will fall out
My teeth will rot
I'll grow fat
Become Republican
And then at last
My body will be done working
And fail me
As I failed it so so many times before
I can't blame it
It's vacation will be my death
A vacation well earned
Because -

My body did it's job
So why didn't I?

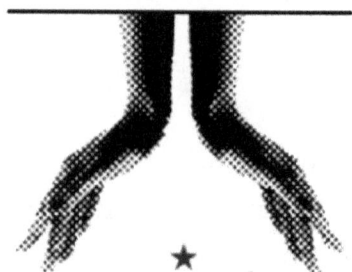

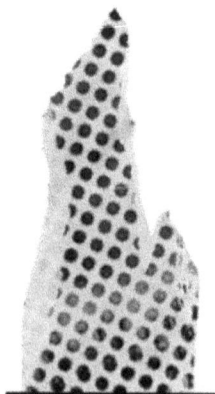

MEMORY

I can't cut myself open and have it pour out of
me like blood
And I can't think it out
Review and revision aren't my strong suits
Art is maliciously spontaneous for me
Fully based in unusually misplaced emotion
Demanding forcefully to have absolutely no
introduction or build up
"Here we are now – relegate us!"
Basically;
Words just have to come
But lately they are truant
I don't mind their absence
Room to breath is nice
But I do sometimes fear
Age and stability will get the better of me
Age I can't control
No one can
And we've been trying to for so damn long
From Ponce De León to plastic surgery

Didn't work for Ponce
Didn't work for Kim K
Won't work for me
But stability -
Stability I can control to some degree
Unfortunately.

Is this pattern of self sabotage worth it?
To stay creative
hip,
trendy,
(figuratively) young,
"cool" in the "scene" and
almost,
not quite,
but almosttt
happy.
Is that how it has to be?
Is there no other way?
Am I stupid?
Wrong?
Silly goose?
Stupid wrong silly goose?

Either way -
I'm quitting my job and getting drunk
tomorrow
Maybe I'll write a new poem or song
My masterpiece or manifesto
But either way
For at least a few minutes
I won't remember this horrible moment
of clarity

BONER

Sometimes I wish I could shoot off the tips of
my fingers like bullets
Sometimes I wish I could rip my spine out and
crack it like a whip
Sometimes I wish I could take my whole rib
cage out and use it like those over the top
medieval torture devices
I wish I could
use my body
in unconventional lethal ways
The same way I can use my mind
in unconventional lethal ways
Like when I think about it all
And choose to write it down
About how I hate
What I hate
Who I hate
How it's dark
How I"m lonely
How it's dark
etc etc etc

I don't know how to end this "poem" But I
thought it would be funny
Or at least a happier ending
To make some kind of joke

I don't know

Something something something
Boner

HELLO

Sometimes if I see someone in the distance
And I don't feel like being seen
I hope that they can't see me
But I know they can
Because I can see them
And then I think about my eyesight
And how bad it is
What can they see about me
That I can't see about them from this far away?
I try to comfort myself by thinking
They're eyesight might be worse than mine
Which is not likely –
But maybe
Maybe they're blind
Or are they as lost as I am?

Closer

Not able to tell much at this point
Mostly just hair length and clothes

Which aren't reliable enough indications to
feel safe
But I do what I can
As I suppose they are

Closer

Colors become more vivid here
Warm or cold
How will this go
What do they already know about me
Male - they know that
Beard - they know that
Earth tones - they know that

Closer

This is the most pivotal
Young or old
Carrying anything
Walking a dog or child

Glasses and headwear
Sneakers or sandals

Closer

Movement type
Confident or cautious
Are they doing the same to me?
I've come to terms with being this big and
scary
Bearded because I hate my chin
Usually frowning – occasionally because I hate
my chin
Usually talking to myself unless I remember to
catch it
Usually aloof with my bouncing walk
It looks dumb I've been told

Closer

Facial expression
I follow suit with theirs

Are we making eye contact today?

Closer

The game of cerebral chicken is well underway
Like hunting
Am I the prey or predator here?
I never get to truly decide myself
Does that make them in charge
Or are they as lost as I am?

Closer
Closer
Closer

"Hey!"
"Hi."
"Hello..."

Shit I messed it up...

where am i?

"Plan B is just Plan A with a raincoat."

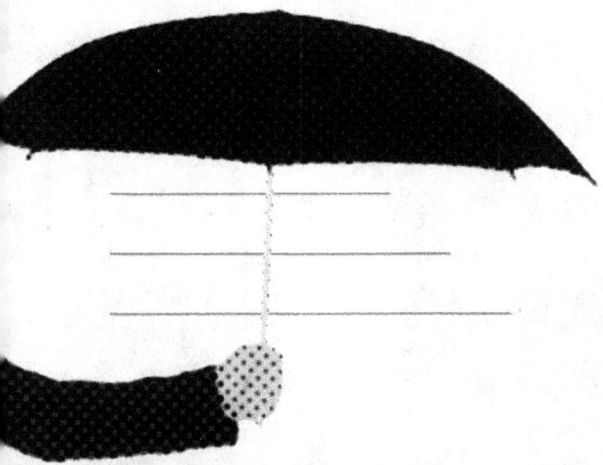

J. HOL

THE LOVELY LITTLE ASTRONAUT

The lovely little astronaut
He sits and sits and thinks
The lovely little astronaut
Wants a smile not a wink
The lovely little astronaut
He's got a lot of fear
The lovely little astronaut
He doesn't want to be here

CAREFREE

I want to be happy
I want to be carefree
I want to know what it's like
To do something
And not fail miserabyl

KIT-KATS

And when you said you wanted a break
And I made that joke about Kit-Kats
You didn't find it -
Funny
Punny
Or anything at all
You just left
But thats okay
Because if you don't laugh at my Kit-Kat jokes
Maybe it's not meant to be
Because I'll never stop making stupid jokes
Because stupid jokes make me happy
And help me
Deal with gravity
But maybe one day
I'll be like a Snickers
"SATISFIED"
With my life (no)
With my wife (no)

With three kids and a baby on the way (god no
fuck that)
Anyway -
I miss you
Even though you don't like my jokes
I miss you
And the way
You'd roll your eyes to say
That's not
Funny
Punny
Or anything at all
But you would smile
And i would smile
And that was nice

I SAW A BIRD ON DuPONT ST

A bird flies over the desert sky
And I feel nothing
But it's not always about me
I'm not meant to feel anything
The bird doesn't fly for me
Just as I don't walk for it
But –
Her wings stretched staunchly
The bird flies for herself
I do not walk for myself
I walk to satiate the holes in my pockets for
money
I walk to satiate the holes in my stomach for
hunger
I walk to satiate the holes in my judgment for
alcohol
I walk for the will of powers I do not love nor
intend to ever love
The sidewalk is prison
My feet accomplices
The bird may fly

for pleasure
She may fly
for pain
I will never know
Because I'll never get a chance to stop walking
To ask her

FOR THE WOMAN IN THE WHEELCHAIR AT THE PHOENIX SKY HARBOR AIRPORT

It was just you and I

The only two titans in this arena of hellos and goodbyes

I was unsure of what I suppose to do

But for reasons obvious enough I reached the escalator faster than you did

I stepped on

I had risen about 3 feet before you rolled your way to the device

I watched as you sat at the bottom

Staring at the robotic steps as they flowed upward

You looked sad

You looked confused

You looked lost

You looked sad

I stared at you

Slowly being whisked further away Standing rigid

Slowly taken

Magnetically drawn

I know what we were both thinking:

What's your next move?
-
How the fuck are you going to do this?
-
Oh shit.

You sat
You looked up at me
You looked sad
You looked confused
You looked lost
You looked sad
Out of sheer tension-breaking awkwardness

I smiled.

I'm sorry
I regret that smile
It must have seemed quite smug
As you rolled away defeated

THE RETURN POLICY ISN'T STATED

Turning your life into a permanent party
Bending your own rules
Supplying your own logic
Thinking you have rules and/or logic at all
Creating a world without

~~~~ Without without withou t ~~~~

The call and response of a healthy well
adjusted adult

~~~~ Without without witho u t ~~~~

Listen to it echo
In your big dumb fucking head

~~~~ Without without with o u t~~~~

Without any of it
At all
Nothing to lose

Nothing to spare
Except the constant
Supply and demand of the liver
Drinking is mandatory
Failure is fun
You don't have to think – at all
Until alone
You will watch
The tindered house
Meet the flame of the hour
Oh comedy
tragedy
dignity
The big nothing is infinite
And will swallow you whole honey

ROCK BOTTOM

I've hit rock bottom
And it feels great
I've got rock bottom
And I can't relate
To you
To me
Or to anything at all
I've hit rock bottom
And I'm building a wall
Filling in the cracks
With compliments
Sealing them softly
With my regrets
Because I can't go up
I can't climb that high
I've hit rock bottom
But I don't want to die

MR. PEELERS WOODS

When I was about 8 I made friends with a
mentally challenged boy named Trevor
His disability was slight
But at times it would show
I didn't understand it
Or mind it
Then and now
We played outside in the woods a lot with
sticks and rocks
Trevor introduced me to "The Lord of the
Rings"
The books, the movies, the GameCube game
that accompanied them -
The whole lot
We became obsessed together and frequently
reenacted our favorite scenes
Despite our small statues more fit for a hobbit I
usually played the part of Aragon
Trevor usually played the part of Legolas
I found a big long stick and made a duct tape
handle
A glorious sword

Trevor found a curved stick and used a
shoelace to make a bow
We salvaged my mother's broken kitchen knife
and duct taped it to a small stick to make an
arrow that would actually stick into the trees,
and our legs if we weren't careful
It was fun
We'd go into the woods and ruthlessly beat
down broken logs and hanging branches
I told him we were training for the big battle,
like at the end of "Return of the King"
Against the monstrous Orcs to reclaim our
rightful kingdom
We trained and trained –
Those branches never saw it coming
We bashed and slashed our path through their
woods
Nothing was safe
We were training to win
The fate of everything imaginable (literally)
rested on us

And then –
The day of the big battle came
We went to a different section of the woods
Behind old man Mr. Peelers house
The woods behind his house were denser and
unkept
He was too old for the upkeep
And they seemed quieter
More gradious
We marched -
Me with my duct taped sword

Trevor with his shoe laced bow
Step by step
Side by side
We called out real commands to imaginary
armies
Gave impromptu speeches of bravery and
brotherhood
Sang our war cries
Until finally
We reached a small clearing
Our battlefield
I stormed in
Clutching my sword
Swinging wildly smashing every branch in
sight
Wood chips and dust whirled around me
"FORWARD MEN!"
I yelled out
I looked back to Trevor
He had a puzzled look on his face

His bow hung by his side instead of drawn
"Come on Trevor! I need your help!"
He stood
"It's just branches. Where are the monsters?"
He asked
"Right here!"
I screamed, beginning to swing furiously again
"That's just a tree. I thought we were fighting
the Orcs today."
And with that –
Trevor turned and left
Leaving me alone in the woods behind old
man Mr. Peelers house
Had he actually expected us to fight a real
army of Orcs?
Like in the books
Or the movies
Or the more pixelated version from the
GameCube game that accompanied them
I was confused, but I continued to fight
The battle raged on

I flopped and flailed until every branch my
skinny arms could reach had fallen
Every dead log was beaten senseless
Every low hanging leaf shredded
Broken on the forest floor
I sat down and marveled at my work
I thanked my men
Fashioning some wiry weeds into a crown
Crowned myself the true king –
then turned around and marched home
triumphantly
I was out of breath
But
I felt accomplished
I felt good
I felt proud and happy and gay
Even if Trevor had abandoned me
We had won
I had won

But now
When I think about that
I often wonder
Who was less based in reality?
Trevor, for expecting two 8 years olds to fight
an actual army of Tolkien's most heinous
beings
Or me
Bashing a duct taped stick against trees for
hours, yelling orders to an army that was never
there
And thinking this made me king
And thinking I was doing anything at all
Sweating
Panting
Bleeding

And thinking I had won

King of the nothing

GOD BLESS

I was laying on her bed
Soundly
Comfortably
My head tilted back
My arms over my head
My legs crossed
Lounging
Like I was on some beautiful international
beach I'll never get an opportunity to actually
visit
She was sitting beside my legs
Half on them
It didn't hurt
Rifling through a wooden box
Taking out old used bags of powder
Sifting through them
Looking for every inch of the white gold
untouched by our insides

SNIFFFFFFFF
"Found some"

I didn't reply
Just smiled
That's all I needed
That's all she needed

"Want some"
This time I will reply -
"Of course"

She holds the fragmented bag up to my face as
I sit up

SNIFFFFFFFF
A sudden charge
I open my eyes for the first time again
I missed her face
God bless this drug
God bless this girl
And our carnal charge towards impending
doom
Or whatever we are headed for -
God bless

UPPISH

I don't know why
I aggressively segment my life by tragedy
Accurately too
I remember it was April 22, 2021 when my
van / home broke down
And it was the following June, June 10th, I
was diagnosed with cancer
But now -
I'm driving my little house around beautiful
California
Care-free
Cancer-free
And I have no idea when that all happened
Just did
What I mean is –
I want to remember
The good
I want partition my life by stride
Like –
Nice, the open road - also affordable housing
Instead of -
Shit, I'm homeless and stationary

I want to remember -
Fuck yeah – no more cancer
Instead of -
Fuck no – one less testicle
Anyway –
Is it pessimism
Nihilism
Apathy
And if it is any of these things
I'll need the other shoe to drop
Like a fucking rocket
And bring the sun
As I stand here

Completely naked
In my little thundercloud
I don't know why I'm naked
But it means more that way
Although –
I did find a quarter today
So now I'm that much closer to affording
laundry
Things are looking up...
Things are looking upper...
Things are looking uppish...

That's it –
Things are looking at least -

uppish

entertain us!

"If at first you don't succeed – fuck it!"

QUARANTINED

Right now
I'm stuck walking on the sidewalk of a busy
Arizona street between two people making
very passionately / very personal / very loud
phone calls
Cars are passing quickly -
I can't cross the street
Four lanes
Without a crosswalk in sight
No alcoves or driveways to stow away into
So –
I'm threading my distance
Trying to stay balanced between the two
Bits of conversation float in

"Baby come on now it..."
from man one

"...but how did this..."
from man two

"...never again I..."
man one again

"...well...fuck and"
man two is maddddd

"...I SAID NEVER AGAIN!"
oh shit

Back and forth and forth and back
I am a fly on a wall to simultaneous individual
apocalypses
Neither of them seem to notice me
Neither seem to care
As I am awkwardly quarantined
Between disasters
I should be thankful I'm not one of them
Nothing is changing for me
Nothing is bad or good in this moment
Nothing is sad or happy in this moment
I am as balanced as my stride
I am the strangest life I'm living
But for once

I am not the worst on screen

8/12/2018

And when you smiled
I tore that page out of my notebook
That said I hated everything

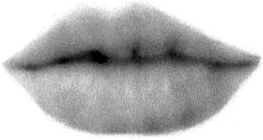

CURE PORN

I don't like porn
Not morally
I don't care –
fuck on camera – that's fine with me
Whatever
But it just doesn't do it for me
Never has really
So I don't watch porn much
But if I did
And I was to be in one
Not like **IN** it per say
But as a director
(Which – sidebar – first of all is a horrible idea
How can you direct something you
(1) don't know anything about
(2) don't even like
Anyway –)
If I were to direct –
I'd want the song "Close to Me" by The Cure to
be playing in the background
It's the seventh track off "The Head on the
Door" album

And it's simply a really tender song, in my
opinion
And I think it would make a heartfelt
pornography
It's also a little dorky with the synth in the
beginning
And I think sex is inherently dorky looking
Flopping around and poking stuff
You know?
*(And – sidebar – yes sex is dorky flopping and
poking*
*I've said this before and some knob always has to
chime in with "ha bud, I think ya doin sex
wrong"*
No, no I'm not
*You **knob***
*In its most basic form - sex is literally flopping
and poking – gay//straight//???*
Whatever
It's true so fuck off
*You **KNOB***
Anyway –)

So yeah – I think that would be a real great
porn
I might even watch it
Honestly The Cure has a lot to offer the porn
community
For example:

"Boys Don't Cry" could be used for some kind
of aggressive gay porn or a female dominatrix
type deal
"Friday I'm in Love" easily could be turned into
a porny parody
"Friday I'm in Love, Saturday We Funkin"
"Head in the Door" obviously a glory hole
reference
"Pictures of You" masturbation duh
And "Just like Heaven" seems pretty self
explanatory

I think these would all make great pornograpy
and would bring about some intriguing art

Not to mention the merging of two prime communities

Right now all they have in common is leather

But yeah I guess I'll just say and print this "poem" -

until someone more equipped in porny things hears me and makes it happen

I'm an advocate

Are you out there?

Cure porn!

Cure porn!

Cure porn!

TRUE STORY

The walls closing in
Endless and nameless isles
The people
The people gather in drones
Words seemingly in another language than my
own pester my very existence
The chatter of rebellious machines singing
their war cries

_____**Beep**

_____**Beep**

_____**Beep**

Closing in
As more people rush the door
A sea of innumerable options, with no end in
sight
-

And THAT is what it feels like shopping at
Whole Foods when I'm stoned

BRAD

was the kind of guy who thought everything he
had to say was of the utmost importance
Always this way -
I'd listen
And nod
And smile
And tune out
Think about
my life
my love
my disdain
And then
Brad would look at me
And say:
"Well what do you think?"

And I'd say:
"Sounds good Brad."

And then it was back to -
listen

nod
smile
tune
think
life
love
disdain

"Sounds good Brad."

Now,
I am sure
you know Brad
And if you don't
You'll meet Brad
He is everywhere
In Kansas
In Kentucky
In Rhode Island
In Chicago
In China
In Rome
In Spain
In McDonalds

In Dubai
In your bed right now
In LA
In Alaska
In Walmart
In Johannesburg
And of course –
At work

And when you do
Just like I -
You will
listen
nod
smile
tune
life
love
disdain

"Sounds good Brad."

And Brad will do the rest

WRITE A POEM ABOUT REBELLION

no.

get it...?

THE LITTLE THINGS

I think it's important to learn a little bit from
everyone you meet
To constantly evolve
Reevaluate
Reinvent
I think, in a way, that's really what my ideal
definition of humanity is:
Evolution
Very original I know
Call me Charlie Darwin I guess
But yes –
Taking those experiences and molding yourself
into a better person by learning a little bit from
everyone
Is important

Like my grandfather
He taught me to stick to my guns

In his case that meant literal guns
He was very Republican
Bit of a gun nut
But of course
Metaphorically
Stick to my guns

Or my good friend Jake
He always thinks things through and finds a
compromise for any problem
He finds the common ground where everyone
can agree
So everyone wins
Also he hates guns
(sorry grandpa)

Or the stranger in the bathroom at the Phoenix
Sky Harbor Airport
We were sitting next to each other in the stalls

and he airdropped a picture of his shit to me
mere moments after the maiden plop
Just -

pop

And there it was
in all it's glory
The picture not the shit
Well...

pop..

You decided what that noise sounds like I
guess

Anyway –
When you learn from people you grow
You become more well rounded
Dare I say –
A better person

Now in times of trouble
I stick to my guns
In times of insurmountable problem
I look for compromise
And when I find myself on the front lines of
the porcelain thrones next to strangers
Of course -
I airdrop them a picture of my shit

Because life is about the little things
Or the big things
Depends on what I ate

OUR FRIEND THE FLY

As I sit in my living room on the couch
I am drunk
As I do most nights
The living room being my "sober up" tank
Before I enter the bedroom hosted by my
sleeping beauty
Thankfully thoroughly sleeping by this time

As I sit in my living room on the couch
And think about how I can't even say the
alphabet backwards sober
I am joined by my usual late night companion
The cat
He doesn't judge or treat me differently
He wants pets all the same
He wants tummy rubs and chin scratches
He wants to see me
Not because he is fully awake
But because I am

As I sit in my living room on the couch
I am joined by a new friend tonight –
A fly

He buzzes and darts on the windowsill
Unaware he is crashing a nightly ritual
I don't take issue
Fly all you want
It's your namesake
The cat does not share my opinion
He starts by acknowledging his presents with
what can only be described as fluttered gargles
The cat can meow just fine
But this sound is exclusive to flies and similar
creatures
I don't know if it's supposed to sound
threatening or inviting to them
But to me
It just sounds weird

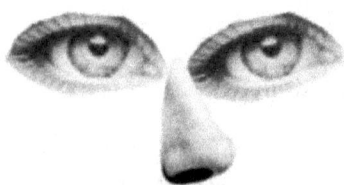

As I sit in my living room on the couch
The cat leaps from my lap
Clawing at walls he should know he can't
climb
To play or to kill is still undefined
That line rhymes

As I sit in my living room on the couch
The cat will not stop
His fluttered gargles become louder
As he scrapes the poorly painted wood
I get to Q in the reverse alphabet before I
decide to help
Together we can win

As I stand in my living room on the couch
I am holding the cat and aiming him, so he can
catch the fly
He's egging me on with his gargles
The fly doesn't seem to be too worried
He dodges his paws with ease
Never going far enough to make me get off the
couch

Which I appreciate

As I jump in my living room on the couch
He closes in on the fly
His movements timed with mine like we've
been doing this for years
An unlikely fly hunting team
A superfluous answer to a common problem
When I go down he rests
When I spring up he attacks
Paws flying as he sings our war cry
The fly is within our grasp
It won't be long now

As I soar higher and higher in my living room
on the couch
We are closer than ever
The fly is tiring we can tell
And we —

"What the hell are you doing!"

A voice cuts through us all

"Uh..."

How would I even explain this –

It's 5am
The cat is falling asleep in my arms
Our friend the fly is now nowhere to be seen
He must have taken the hint
Did we win?
Does it matter?
I think I'm sober now

QUESTION 4

Using the answers provided below; complete the sentence: Comedy Means _____

A. Comedy means I hate you

B. Comedy means I love you

C. Comedy means I hate myself

D. Comedy means I love myself

E. Comedy means I hate to love myself

F. Comedy means I love to hate myself

G. Comedy means a subjective form of entertainment made strictly to relax my mind and ease all the pity I place upon my privileged self in order to interact with the world around me and be accepted by it even when I do everything else within my power to deny I want love or acceptance at all

H. Comedy means *insert fart noise here*

I. Comedy means a human oriented oral tradition passed down one dick joke at a time

J. Comedy means self loathing masked as self deprecation masked as self pity masked as self bemusement masked as self acceptance masked as self love

K. Comedy means tragedy

L. Comedy means die young

M. Comedy means help

N. Comedy means help

O. Comedy means FOR FUCKS SAKE THIS IS A CRY FOR HELP

Q. Comedy means you didn't realize I skipped P

R. Comedy means fuck it let's just do the whole alphabet at this point, well except the P we skipped for the sake of that joke

S. Comedy means stalling for time... T. Comedy means...uhhh...

U. Comedy means surviving through past traumatic experiences and making it out hilariously alive

V. Comedy means connecting through past traumatic experiences and making it out hilariously alive

W. Comedy means...yeah what he said

P. Comedy means fuck your rules I'll put the P wherever I want thank you very much

X. Comedy means none of the above

Y. Comedy means all of the above

Z. Comedy means I'm still here

Answer: ___

PLEASE READ THIS AT MY FUNERAL

Sometimes when I go to bed I think about
Or rather
Half heartedly (death) wish
I would die in my sleep
Edgy, I'm aware
But I do
Obviously it's a depression thing
#justdepressionthangz
But also it would save me all the work of dying
Never mind making the choice for me
Which is arguably (dependent upon how well
you plan) the hardest part
I'd say freedom is overrated but that seems
insensitive
But in my –
#justdepressionthangz
brain, it seems that way sometimes
Freedom is the prison of choice and choice is
the prison of thought and thought is the prison
of overthinking etc etc
Describing freedom as a prison feels

oxymoronic
But I hope you can understand a little
So yeah –
I'd just die in my sleep
No choices – no thinking – no prisons
Die
That's it
A freak medical accident
Like I've had this big ol tumor in my head this
whole time
Clunking around doing –
#justtumorthangz
And last night it had just had enough of my
shit

"SHUT IT DOWN!!"
the tumor would yell

"Aye aye captain!"
my cancer drunk brain would reply

And that'd be it
I'd die just like that
All at once
No pain no plan no hospital no light at the end
of the ever-present tunnel
Die
That's it
They would say I went peacefully
That would comfort them
Ease the grief
Because people would be sad
I'm not arrogant but I'm not delusional either
(maybe a bit delusional)
Either way, I am aware
I am loved alive
Friends, a girlfriend, family, a cat
Random old people that still read newspapers
who would say
"Oh what a shame, so young."

While wiping prune juice off their wrinkly lips
They would all miss me
A lot
I know I know I know
They would cry and talk about how I lit up
rooms and my smile was infectious How I
loved to laugh and played by my own rules
...*groan*
Maybe some of my friends would meet my
mom and share a story I never got around to
telling her
Maybe they'd cremate me and spread my ashes
over a fucking Dairy Queen –
#justqueenthangz
Who knows
Point is
I am loved alive
I get that
But to be fair

I think I would be loved not alive as well
And if I died in my sleep
Dealt the final blow by Captain Brain Tumor
No one could blame me
Be mad or torn
Even know -
That I think about these things outside of the
realm of a peaceful sleepy aneurysm
And I choose not to do anything except wish
for the occasional fucking brain tumor because
of all of these people
Call it liability or love
Honestly I don't know

I feel guilty for writing this
Please read this at my funeral
I don't light up rooms

You do

_____
_____
_____
_____

outro –

"You are allowed to be oh so simple."

_____
_____
_____
_____

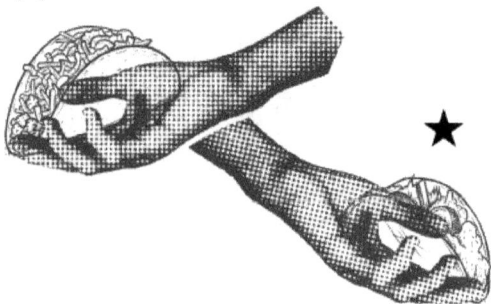

DIE HAPPY

I want to walk around in a grape field

I want to drink four milkshakes at once

I want to jump really high and fall really hard

I want to hit rock bottom and keep digging

I want to know why

I want to buy something stupid off the
television like it's 1997

I want to learn French just to piss off the
French

I want all the answers

I want to eat comically large submarine
sandwiches in a public park

I want to dream again

I want to bleach my hair then shave it all off

I want to realize my hopes

I want to fill a briefcase with tacos and walk
around wearing a suit and sunglasses acting
suspicious and when someone asks me what
I'm doing I'll hastily open the briefcase give
them a mangled taco and say:

"it's just business."

then run away

I want to be able to separate my "funny"
thoughts from my "real" ones
I want to blur the line between the two and
walk it forever
I want to be fashionably late to an annual orgy
I want to able to tell what I'm actually capable
of so I'm neither disappointed or disappointed
some more
I want to manage my emotions as a human
and as an adult
I want to learn
I want to grow
I want to learn and grow in directions I like -

instead of how I'm economically
emotionally academically or mentally
forced to
I want everything
I want nothing
I won't die alone
But I might not die happy
But I'll sure as shit
Die trying
I hope you do too
I hope you're happy
I hope you're trying
If you want to do any of these things too
Just let me know

See ya around ~

About the Author

J. Hol (he/they) is a writer and musician originally from Pawtucket, RI. His work primarily focuses on life on the road, struggles with mental illness, and laughing with the nihilism of the 21st century. He likes pizza and has been a featured in numerous independent publications such as –
Scissortail Quarterty,
The Sour Collective Zine,
Anytown Zine,
High AF Magazine,
The Latte Edit,
Cajun Mutt Press,
and G-Zine.

All these small indie publishers are still going strong and you should check them out.
Do it.

Instagram:: @soxsuxpolkfunk
Bandcamp:: https://soxsux.bandcamp.com/

Thanks

www.ingramcontent.com/pod-product-compliance
Lightning Source LLC
Chambersburg PA
CBHW071232090426
42736CB00014B/3060